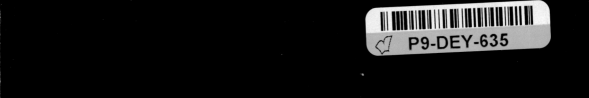

UNCHAIN
THE ELEPHANT

*Reframe Your Thinking
to Unleash Your Potential*

Erik Wahl

Editing by: Alice Patenaude

Photo Credits
Cover: Anup Shah/Getty Images; David Schrader/Thinkstock; IvanNikulin/Thinkstock
Internal: page 1, Anup Shah/Getty Images; pages 2–3, Anna Omelchenko/Shutterstock; pages 4–5, David Schrader/Thinkstock, IvanNikulin/Thinkstock, zizar2002/Thinkstock; pages 8–9, javarman/Shutterstock; page 18, oksix/Thinkstock; page 21, Lora-Sutyagina/Thinkstock; pages 22–23, ndphoto/Shutterstock; pages 26–27, Angelo Lano/Thinkstock; page 29, IvanNikulin/Thinkstock; page 31, Maggy Meyer/Shutterstock; pages 32–33, Ximagination/Thinkstock; pages 36–37, AJP/Shutterstock; page 38, Kesu01/Thinkstock; page 41, Mariusz Prusaczyk/Thinkstock; pages 42–43, rob_lan/Thinkstock; pages 48–49, Oleg Znamenskil/Shutterstock; page 53, Stayer/Shutterstock; pages 56–57, ZwartFotografie/Thinkstock; pages 58–59, Richard du Toit/Getty Images; pages 64–65, Andrzej Kubik/Shutterstock; pages 66–67, Andrew Parkinson/Getty Images; page 69, Lora-Sutyagina/Thinkstock; page 73, VikZa/Thinkstock; page 78, Lora-Sutyagina/Thinkstock; page 83, Lora-Sutyagina/Thinkstock; page 84, kasto80/Thinkstock; pages 86–87, Fly Traveler/Thinkstock; pages 88–89, ndphoto/Shutterstock

Published by Simple Truths, an imprint of Sourcebooks, Inc.
P.O. Box 4410, Naperville, Illinois 60567-4410
(630) 961-3900
Fax: (630) 961-2168
www.sourcebooks.com

Printed and bound in China.
OGP 10 9 8 7 6 5 4 3 2 1

Foreword

I'm a big fan of Erik Wahl. I saw him deliver the commencement address for Grand Canyon University in Phoenix, and his presentation blew everyone away—students, faculty, and staff.

Erik's message in *Unchain the Elephant* is simple: to fully experience all life has to offer, we need to break free from our chains and rediscover our inner creativity and passion. I think the book will resonate with you. It definitely resonates with me. Why?

Our company has a leadership training program called Situational Self Leadership. In the class, we talk about assumed constraints—beliefs we all have, based on past experience, that limit our current and future experiences. Using a similar chained elephant analogy, we teach participants that in order to take personal responsibility for their situation and be effective self-leaders, they must challenge their assumed constraints.

Whether you work in a concert hall, an art studio, a manufacturing plant, or a corporate office, you possess an internal creative intelligence that may not have been expressed since you were young. Some people choose to explore this creative side by using paint; some, music; some, words; and some, ideas. Think about it—if you felt free to express your creative genius, what would it look like?

Thanks, Erik, for challenging us to get out of our own way, face our self-limiting beliefs, and embrace our hidden creativity. This book is a much-needed kick in the pants!

Ken Blanchard,
chief spiritual officer of the Ken Blanchard Companies
and coauthor of The One Minute Manager

Unchain the

Elephant

"All the forces in the world are not so powerful
as an idea whose time has come."

–Victor Hugo

Several years ago, I had the privilege to go on safari outside Nairobi, Kenya. As I ventured into the vast, unregulated openness of the Maasai Mara, I experienced life from a completely new perspective. I witnessed the grace of a pack of gazelles, the migration of the wildebeest, and the clever stealth of the cheetah. But the most memorable encounter by far was when I crested a hill and unexpectedly came face-to-face with the overwhelming size and unparalleled raw power of an untamed elephant.

This was not a petting zoo elephant quietly behaving in a crowded room. This enormous elephant was wild and completely unrestrained to explore, to discover, and to enjoy the beauty of its natural habitat. How did this massive, powerful, free creature succumb to a life tethered to a chain in a circus tent?

When an elephant is born into captivity, the owner ties the animal to a tree or post with a thick chain to prevent the 250-pound infant from escaping. During the first few weeks of his life, the small elephant tests the chain that binds him, again and again, in an attempt to free himself and wander as his nature urges him to do. His efforts, however, are no match for the steel links. Over the course of a few weeks, he eventually learns that his resources are no match for the hardiness of the chain. He gives up any further attempts to free himself, and thus relegates himself to life within a small circle.

As an adult elephant conditioned by his past experience, he can now be tethered to a small tree with the thinnest of ropes or, in some cases, no rope at all. He makes no attempts to wander because he carries with him, for life, the belief that he does not possess the power to break the ties that bind him. The adult elephant could easily snap the rope or uproot the tree to which it is attached, but he makes

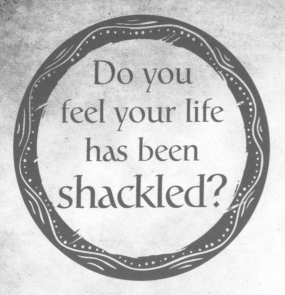

Do you feel your life has been shackled?

no such effort, because early in life, he was taught that true freedom was not available to him. For the remainder of his life, he is tame and nothing like the captivating, powerful creature he was born to be.

Can you sympathize with this elephant? Do you feel your life has been shackled by what you were conditioned to believe when you were young? Maybe the conditioning was even more recent than that.

The time has come to unchain the elephant.

I can only say this because, until I was thirty years old, I was tethered to a tree, not realizing that I had been conditioned to remain quiet and submissive in order to succeed.

I was trapped and entirely unaware of it.

The story begins at a young age when I was told by a well-meaning teacher that *art was not my strength*. Being a disciplined student and wanting to please, I listened. And I became quickly conditioned. I put down my crayons and paintbrushes and did not pick them up again for another twenty years.

In the meantime, I studied hard and learned to play by the rules society expected. Like most, I concluded that strong grades, a college education, and a corporate job with predictable growth would be sufficient. I listened to those in-the-know and accepted the small circle they drew around my future. I then remained in that circle for years, never once attempting to step outside it.

I gave away my freedom at a young age, hoping to gain something secure.

We are all promised the world when we are young, only to discover that when we are older, the offer and opportunities have changed. When we are young, we are told that if we work hard, follow the rules, and put in our time, we will be rewarded with life's "greatest" gift: security. What we don't understand is that when we follow these instructions, we are surrendering an entirely different set of dreams. Following the standard protocol takes away our capacity to think, question, break out, speak up, or wander outside what we are told to do and where we are told to go.

***We are asked to give up the single thing that
makes us unique: our freedom to create.***

Many of you will be unable to understand these seemingly simple words. You may think it doesn't apply to you or feel you already have enough space within the reach of your chain. But you have been blinded. You are not free. To fully live, you must break free of your chains.

How does an elephant break free from its chains?

There are three key moments in life, three unique invitations where we must respond appropriately if we want to unshackle ourselves. **These moments are when we face our *predators*, embrace our *passions*, and rediscover our *packs*.** Each of us will get to experience these key moments, potentially two to three times each. The final question is:

When these moments present themselves, how will you respond?

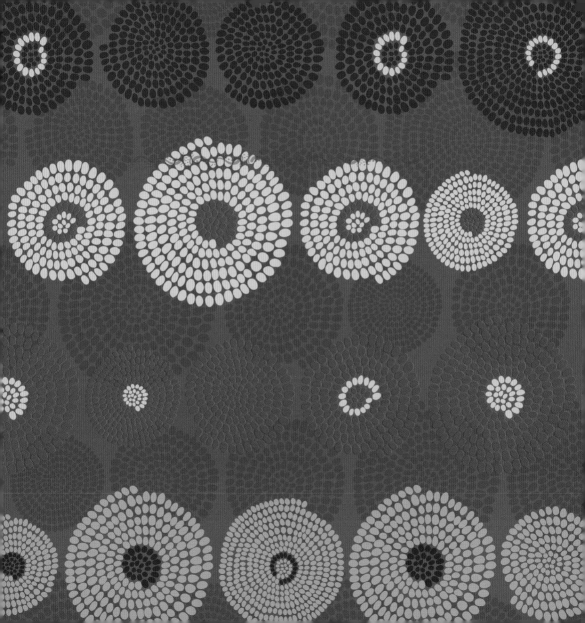

"All change is preceded by crisis."

–Søren Kierkegaard

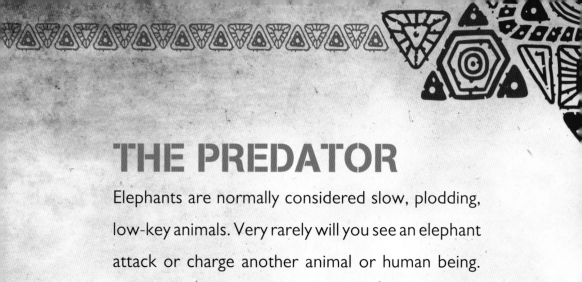

THE PREDATOR

Elephants are normally considered slow, plodding, low-key animals. Very rarely will you see an elephant attack or charge another animal or human being. However, there is one enemy of the elephant that will change its nature—the predator.

The presence of a predator, such as a lion, brings an onset of fear that forces the elephant to make a decision. It can either give up and die, or it can fight. And if that elephant has even the slightest will to live, *it will fight*.

There is no chain capable of holding back a charging elephant.

"When you come out of the storm, you won't be the same person who walked in. That's what this storm's all about."

–Haruki Murakami

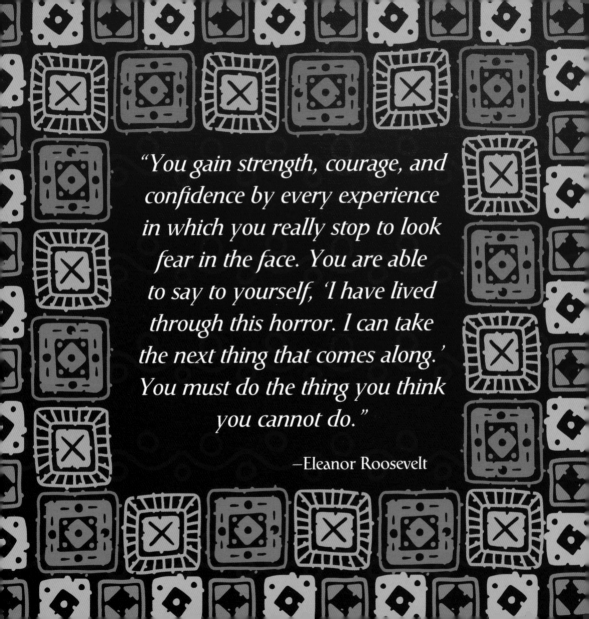

"You gain strength, courage, and confidence by every experience in which you really stop to look fear in the face. You are able to say to yourself, 'I have lived through this horror. I can take the next thing that comes along.' You must do the thing you think you cannot do."

—Eleanor Roosevelt

After ten years in the corporate world, I knew my talents were wasting away inside of me. Despite this realization, I continued to force-feed myself the lies I had been told my entire life. *Put your head down and keep going. Just work harder. Walk the line. Don't question anything.* It wasn't until I was face-to-face with my own predator that I realized what I had to do. In what seemed like an instant, I lost my job, my savings, and my precious security. I had to face my predator of fear. I realized that in order to protect my family, playing it safe was no longer an option. It was time to get drastic, to roll up my sleeves and go start a fight.

The majority of our fear is given to us by the world. Maybe you've been fired, or someone you love has received a terminal diagnosis. Maybe you are facing the results of a terrible decision you made. All of us have faced our predator at one point or another. It is something so horrible it carries the capacity to tear our lives apart. When you are face-to-face with your predator, all the forces in the world are not as powerful as an idea whose time has come. You are forced into a decision: to cower or to fight. You can sit back and be attacked, or lower your head and charge forward.

Turn and face your predator, and fight back.

*"Hardships often prepare ordinary people
for an extraordinary destiny."*

– C. S. Lewis

THE PASSION

Elephants are one of the world's most intelligent species. It has been proven that they show heightened states of grief, learning, play, altruism, self-awareness, and memory.

Their unique ability to solve problems is humanlike. But there still isn't enough brain power to outthink the chain placed on them. And while the idea of a chain holding a giant elephant back is quite sad, it's frightening how similar we are to that elephant.

We are designed to create. However, society tries to dispel this notion at an early age. It tries to make us "play the game" and conform us to its own set of rules. In order to become unchained, you must accept the fact that you exist to create. When you engage in this idea, you express your unique passion.

"You're only given a little spark of madness.
You mustn't lose it."

–Robin Williams

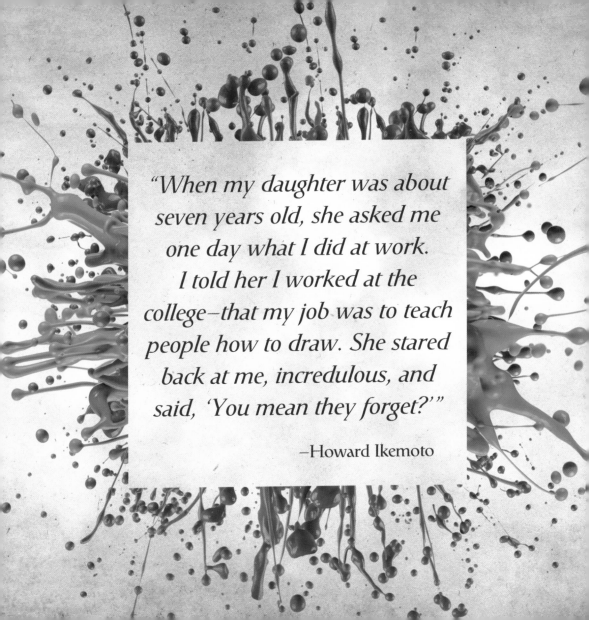

"When my daughter was about seven years old, she asked me one day what I did at work. I told her I worked at the college—that my job was to teach people how to draw. She stared back at me, incredulous, and said, 'You mean they forget?'"

—Howard Ikemoto

Unfortunately, we accept the limitations others place on us as if they were law. It took me twenty years to realize I held the key to my own chains. After coming face-to-face with my predator, I needed something to get excited about, to feel passionate about. I needed something to save me from the dusty, barren world I had become accustomed to.

In my time of self-reflection, frustration, and anger, I became determined to break free from the addiction of security that had lulled the passionate version of me to sleep. By intentionally going against the grain of this addiction, the young artist in me was reawakened. I poured myself into my own new ideas and writings, and, with reckless abandon, spent my free time pursuing my art. I had rediscovered my passion.

When you lose your desire to create, you end up settling, which eventually leads to unhappiness. This unhappiness opens the door to a fog of deterioration that seeps into your soul, leading to a complete loss of your personal freedom and your distinct fingerprint on this world. Remember, you were given something unique that you were created to do. Discover and explore it. You have it inside of you. *Now go find it!*

"An amazing thing happens when you get honest with yourself and start doing what you love, what makes you happy. Your life literally slows down. You stop wishing for the weekend. You stop merely looking forward to special events. You begin to live in each moment and you start feeling like a human being. You just ride the wave that is life, with this feeling of contentment and joy. You move fluidly, steadily, calm and grateful. A veil is lifted, and a whole new perspective is born."

—Jes Allen

THE PACK

Elephants are naturally very social animals. In the wild, they travel in packs and enjoy teaching and learning from each other. They find strength in numbers when

predators attack. However, in captivity, they are often left alone. If you are going to unchain yourself, you must rediscover your pack, because you cannot survive on your own.

Art saved me from the lifeless existence I had accepted in the corporate world and simultaneously led me to a group of people from whom I could draw strength. One of the greatest blessings to come from my art-driven rehab was my association with a pack of creative and passionate artists. I studied under mentors and joined discussions with others who chose to unchain themselves and roam free. I met amazing individuals who shared my passions. This pack became my new testing ground to experiment and play. Here, I was motivated when I felt empty and celebrated when I finally started to find my success.

"People inspire you, or they drain you—
pick them wisely."

–Hans F. Hansen

Benjamin Franklin found his pack. He nicknamed the group his "Junta." They met to discuss ideas, inventions, and the new business plans required to form America in its earliest days as an independent nation. All of this occurred over beers at the local pub. In the 1920s, Paris was the location where Picasso, Hemingway, Stein, Dalí, and Fitzgerald gathered. They created an environment of inspiration and mind-bending innovation that eventually became known as Modern Art.

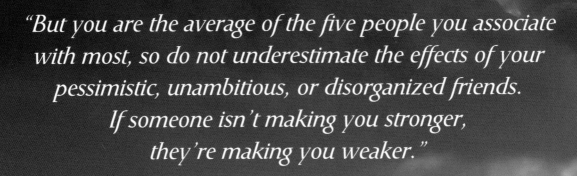

"But you are the average of the five people you associate with most, so do not underestimate the effects of your pessimistic, unambitious, or disorganized friends. If someone isn't making you stronger, they're making you weaker."

–Timothy Ferriss

Choose to **unchain** yourself.

Your pack exists. By facing your predator and adopting your passion, you will be ready to join your own pack.

In every story, there is an inciting incident—a moment that changes everything. Often, it's a moment forced by the world around us, or a decision that you, the main character, choose to act upon. This decision is before you like a key. You must choose to grab hold of it, not knowing precisely what doors it will open. Only you can make that choice.

In the end, you must choose to unchain yourself and wander into the frontier of your new future.

I've given you the key.

NOW GO.

Face your predator. Choose not to cower. Choose instead to rise up and charge. Your freedom begins when you fight back.

Chase your passion. Pick up your paintbrush. Pick up a pen and start writing. Play your instrument. Your freedom grows when you pursue your deepest happiness.

Join your pack. Listen to the wolves howling in the night and take off to join them. Your freedom is solidified when you are finally with your people.

The universe is kind enough to offer us multiple opportunities to pick up these keys, but only you have the ability to break free from your chains. This choice is in your hands.

You are not a quiet little mouse.

You are not a victim of your circumstances.

You are no longer a prisoner.

You do not belong to your chains.

You are a mighty elephant.

You are the most powerful thinking being on the planet.

Your courage hardens your eyes in the face

of your predators.

Your heart races when you chase the passions
   of your heart.
Your desire to know and be known aligns you
   with your pack of wild misfits.

You are destined to face fear.
You are designed to create.
You are made to enjoy life with others.

**Now go. Unlock your chains. Be powerful.
Roam and be free.**

"*The world is but a canvas to our imagination.*"

–Henry David Thoreau

Erik Wahl:

The Story
Behind the Book

I have not always been an artist, at least not practically speaking. It wasn't until decades after an elementary teacher discouraged me that I finally discovered my own chains and freed myself to be the artist I am today. It took a serious shake-up in order for that to happen.

I was a good student who learned to measure my self-worth and value by the way I was taught—the grades on my report card. I learned to be a rule follower who saw little value in creativity, which offered no clear-cut way to measure my progress.

After getting my college degree, I found a comfortable job that earned a decent salary and a title that made me feel respectable at social gatherings. I religiously followed the standard corporate system—follow the rules, meet the quotas, climb the ladder—and was rewarded with corporate success. But the cost was the loss of a part of me that kept life beautiful, fascinating, and fun. Career stability slowly became a dangerous addiction, keeping me from taking any real risk or pursuing any real adventure.

Though I wouldn't admit it then, after a decade in the business world, I still couldn't kick a certain feeling that my best talents were wasting away inside me. I was successful, but my day-to-day life was less and less satisfying.

In an effort to overcome my lackluster existence, I fed my ego. I bolstered my public image and overextended myself financially to puff up my brand. In truth, I wasn't trying to prove myself to the world. I was trying to prove myself to me.

Then the dot-com bubble burst and my fortress of security crumbled. I lost everything.

It was a gut-wrenching and nauseating experience. I was forced to start my career over at age thirty, with a wife and three children under five years old. I obsessed about my losses every night in bed.

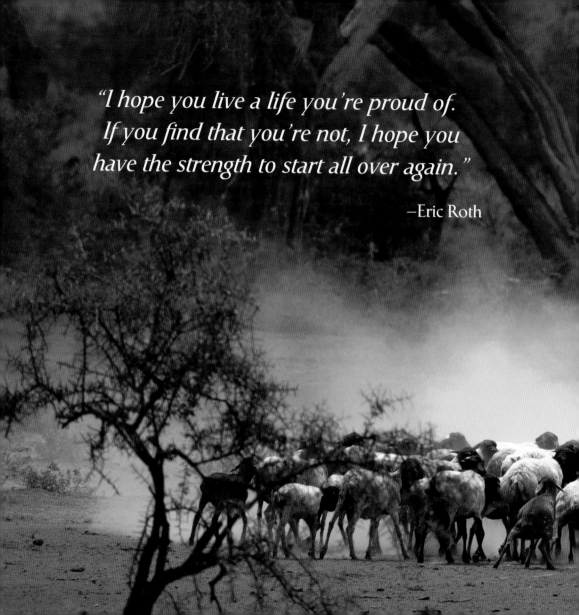

"*I hope you live a life you're proud of. If you find that you're not, I hope you have the strength to start all over again.*"

–Eric Roth

The Predator

in my life had
come out from the shadows
and towered above me.

I spent a lifetime fighting weakness, and my subsequent vulnerability was an unfamiliar, awkward feeling. However, it was this weakness that would serve as my escape hatch to a new life. In short, I was finally pressed to fight with everything in me.

I got real with myself for the first time in a long time. I finally admitted that my days hadn't been inspiring. They paid the bills and gave me a sense of progress. But that progress didn't move me.

This confession woke me from my standardized slumber. I gave myself permission to be a child again.

The Passion inside me

was awakened.

The truth was that I had been seduced into a life of little conviction—a logical, systematic existence. My best talents had been buried beneath well-intentioned, but ultimately lifeless rules, meant to hem me into the corporate fabric.

The existence I thought I controlled turned out to actually control me. My pillars of success were walls that kept me from seeing my own horizon. It was as if I was living in a cabin in the most pristine mountain range in the world, only the cabin didn't have doors or windows. I made do with what was inside the cabin, never realizing that just outside was more beauty, adventure, and meaning in every direction than I could imagine.

Now the cupboards were bare, and I had no more wood to light a fire. My choice was simple: stay inside and starve to death, or get outside the walls and find a way to survive.

I chose to *kick down* the walls of my security and *explore.*

That's when I discovered painting.

With no formal training, I picked up some supplies and poured myself onto a canvas. No rules. No standards. Being messy, spreading paint with brushes and hands, was cathartic. But it was more than therapy. I found painting fascinating and beautiful. It called to me in a way nothing had in years. *I followed the voice.*

The Pack that would
renew my strength and
clarify my path was found.

I started hanging out with local artists—dialoguing and exploring ideas with them. My mind started to expand in every direction. I began to drink in life like a child again.

I started to understand art, not only as a noun (a finished piece of work), but also as a verb (a leaping, diving, daring way of living). Whether I could make it a career remained to be seen. Still, the opportunity to remake myself into something more true seemed a risk worth taking. In fact, it was less risky than returning to who I had been. I dove headlong into rediscovering myself—in particular, that part

of me who longed for exploration without timelines…
imagination without boundaries…execution without rules.

But I wasn't seeing the whole picture before me. The more
I explored the art community, the more I realized that it
also had limitations. While many of the artists I met had
incredible originality and skill, they lacked the training and
tools to make a living. Their creativity did not translate
into creative commerce, primarily because they assumed
that businesses were built on passion and ideas alone. As a

result, these artists often succumbed to the cliché that they were obscure because the world simply didn't understand its need for them.

Having come from a corporate gig, I knew better. But what then was my stance? If I didn't fully buy into corporate conventions or the artistic community, was I a corporate anarchist? An artistic bureaucrat? I found myself caught between an appreciation of corporate know-how and an appreciation of artistic imagination, without full faith in either.

That's when it hit me.

My faith was not

in one or the other.

It was in BOTH.

The realization struck me as an epiphany. I eventually saw that when the artistic sensibilities that drive constant innovation were combined with the practical business strategies that I had learned to apply so effectively, breakthrough was not only possible; it was more frequent and sustainable. I discovered that the character traits that shaped artistic icons like Picasso, Hemingway, and Mozart were the same ones that shaped business titans like Buffett, Jobs, and Branson. I knew if I could distill and teach others those core behaviors, they could become a more positive, potent force in whatever they chose to do. Most importantly, I knew it would free others up to be fully alive.

In the days that followed, I began to organize my thoughts into a presentation I could share with corporate audiences. My new career path was clear: I became a different brand of corporate speaker who, instead of merely reframing the old trains of thought, began challenging companies to "unthink" their traditional ways and venture on to a new frontier governed by business intellect *and* artistic intuition, corporate sense *and* creative sensibility.

To drive home the point, I allowed my art to become a visual metaphor by painting live from the stage during my presentation, coloring each canvas in a matter of three minutes. These sixty-minute presentations, which my epiphany led me to, were far more than my own job opportunity. They were a pathway to a more vibrant, more adventurous, more potent career for anyone willing to rediscover their fearless creativity—their whole, confident, breakthrough identity—and then let it fly. And now, fifteen years later, I can report that millions have found their own paths through a bestselling book called *Unthink* and through over one thousand presentations for organizations like Microsoft, Disney, AT&T, Bristol-Myers Squibb, Honda, and ING.

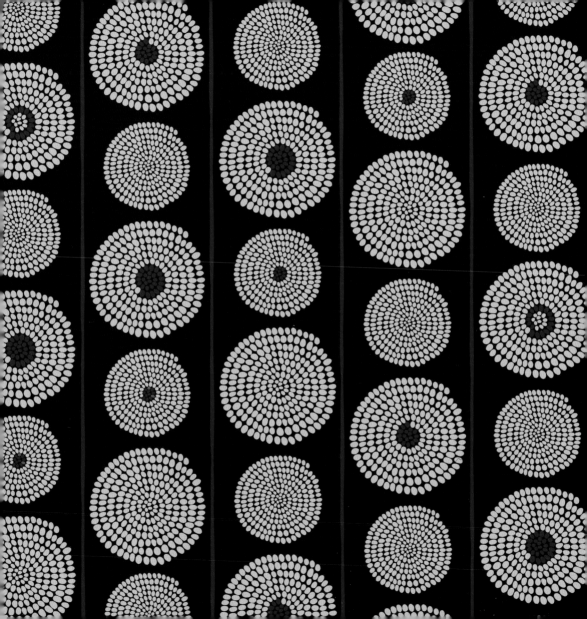

In the end, I realized that our greatest potential isn't reached by conventional, critical thinking alone or by innovative, unconventional thinking alone. Our greatest personal potential is reached when unbridled imagination is applied with critical competence and when business acumen embodies artistic finesse.

That synthesis changed everything I do.

It will do the same for you.

"*In the final seconds before the lights blow out, only you will know whether you've cheated yourself.*"

–Jim Goad

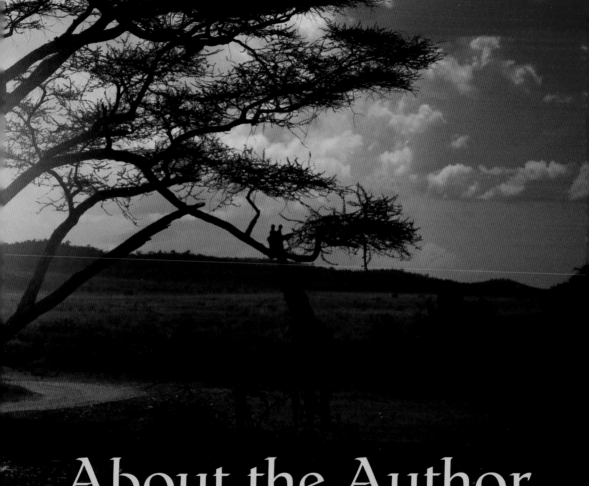

About the Author

Erik Wahl is an internationally recognized graffiti artist, number one bestselling author, and entrepreneur. Erik redefines the term "keynote speaker." Pulling from his history as both a businessman and an artist, he has grown to become one of the most sought-after corporate speakers available today. Erik's onstage painting seamlessly becomes a visual metaphor to the core of his message, encouraging organizations toward profitability through innovation and superior levels of performance. His list of clients includes AT&T, Disney, the London School of Business, Microsoft, FedEx, ExxonMobil, Ernst & Young, and XPRIZE. Erik has even been featured as a presenter at TED, a conference bringing together people from three worlds—technology, entertainment, and design.

Erik's bestselling business book, *Unthink*, was hailed by *Forbes* magazine as "**THE** blueprint to actionable creativity" and by *Fast Company* magazine as "provocative with a purpose." *Unthink* was also named the 2013 "book of the year" by *CEO Reads*.

Erik's understanding of vision was originally born in the school of disappointment. After an eight-year career as a partner in a corporate firm, he became frustrated by the lack of innovative thought and corresponding profits he saw in business. So he set out to challenge companies to change their way of thinking, while simultaneously pursuing his own individual passions. He rediscovered his love for art and now *plays* in the business world by *working* through his art.

Erik's sought-after graffiti artwork has raised millions of dollars for charity and can be seen hanging prominently in executive offices all over the world.

He Is Erik Wahl:

graffiti artist, author, entrepreneur, and philanthropist

Photo by Skip O'Donnell

www.theartofvision.com

WHAT OTHERS ARE SAYING...

"We purchased a Simple Truths gift book for our conference in Lisbon, Spain. We also personalized it with a note on the first page about valuing innovation. I've never had such positive feedback on any gift we've given. People just keep talking about how much they valued the book and how perfectly it tied back to our conference message."

—Michael R. Marcey, Efficient Capital Management, LLC

"The small inspirational books by Simple Truths are amazing magic! They spark my spirit and energize my soul."

—Jeff Hughes, United Airlines

"Mr. Anderson, ever since a friend of mine sent me the 212° movie online, I have become a raving fan of Simple Truths. I love and appreciate the positive messages your products convey and I have found many ways to use them. Thank you for your vision."

—Patrick Shaughnessy, AVI Communications, Inc.